This book is dedicated to my children; Kyle, Briana and Andre. Thank you for loving me unconditionally as an imperfect parent. Thank you for having patience as I learned how to be your mother. You have taught me the meaning of life, love, and happiness. I have learned so much and have gained much joy from watching you grow up. Thank you for helping me grow into the person that I am and will continue to become. You have taught me the true meaning of love.

~   ~   ~   ~

To my Grandma Pickelman, whom I could always count on and who taught me unconditional love, kindness, and patience. She loved my children and me with all of her heart. Grandma Ginny, I will forever cherish all of the memories that I have of you!

~   ~   ~   ~

To my friend Katie White. My soul sister since our paths crossed. You will be greatly missed but never forgotten.

Written by Karri L. Kuzma

Illustrated by Shelby Baxter

Letters on cover by Katie While

Katie was excited to get home from school because her mom promised her that they would have a picnic when she got home. She got off the bus and walked to the house as fast as she could.

It was a very beautiful, warm and sunny day. "Mom, I'm home," she yelled as she ran to the backyard to sit at the picnic table by the old weeping willow tree. She started thinking about her Grandma as she waited for her mom to finish making the food. This was Grandma's favorite place to have lunch in the summertime.

Katie was excited to see what her mom would make. She always made the best lunches. Her favorite lunch was peanut butter and jelly sandwiches shaped like hearts with sliced apples. As she sat there next to the willow tree, enjoying the warm breeze, a willow branch gently caressed her arm and she started thinking about her Grandma. I miss Grandma she thought to herself as she looked at the willow branch.

Katie's mom finally made it outside with the food. She put the plate on the table and sat down. As they sat there, her mom couldn't help but notice that she looked very sad even though she had made her favorite lunch for her. "What's wrong dear?" said mom.

"I miss Grandma," Katie replied as a small tear trickled down her cheek. "I know, even though she's not with us anymore on this earth she is still with us in spirit and, most importantly, in our hearts and memories" said mom.

"What do you mean mom? How is she still here if she's gone?" said Katie. "Grandma loved you very much, and you were a big part of her life, just as much as she was yours," said mom.

Katie's mom explained to her, that even though people we love pass away and we don't get to see them anymore, the memories we make with them while they are here stay in our thoughts each and every day. As long as we continue to remember them, we keep our special ones alive in our hearts.

Her mom told her, "pay attention to the little things and you will see that she is still here with you." Katie asked, "what little things?"

"It could be anything," her mom said, "Just pay attention and you will know. You will see signs and know that she is still watching over you." Excited, Katie ate her last piece of apple and ran into the house to finish her chores and schoolwork.

Later that night as Katie laid in her bed, she couldn't fall asleep. All she could think about was how she missed her grandma and the talk she had with her mom earlier in the day. As she lay there, a bright light kept shining in her eyes. No matter which way she turned it still caught her eye. She got out of bed and went to the window to see what it was.

She looked up into the dark sky where there was one, bright, shining star. The only star in the sky that night. She kept looking around for other stars, but she couldn't find any. This star stood out and seemed much different than any other star that she had seen before. It was the brightest star ever! Grandma had always called Katie her shining little star.

Katie remembered what her mother said and thought Grandma, is that you? This made her very happy. She stared at the star a little longer and then got back into bed.

The thought of her grandma watching over her made her smile and she fell fast asleep.

The next day after school, she went to play in the backyard. As she was swinging, she noticed a beautiful red cardinal that kept flying in circles around her as if it was trying to get her attention. It landed on the swing next to her.

The little red cardinal started flying again and landed on her shoulder. Katie said, "Grandma, is that you?" As the cardinal flew away, Katie had a smile on her face and yelled "I love you Grandma!" then continued to swing.

The next day Katie was helping her mom set the table. They were listening to the radio and Grandma's favorite song came on. They looked at each other and grinned and said at the same time, "Grandma, is that you?" With smiles still on their faces they started dancing around the dining room. Grandma loved to dance to this song whenever she heard it on the radio.

Each day that passed, Katie began to feel better. The sadness she once felt turned into joy. Her tears turned into smiles with the thought of Grandma near. "You have been smiling more lately," said mom. "You were right, Grandma is still here with us, just in different ways. I'm glad we made lots of memories with Grandma," said Katie. "Me too!" said mom. They both smiled and gave each other a big, long hug.

www.ingramcontent.com/pod-product-compliance
Lightning Source LLC
LaVergne TN
LVHW010024070426
835508LV00001B/38